BAJA CALIFORNIA TRAVELS SERIES
General Editors: Edwin Carpenter & Glen Dawson

22

Letter of

LUÍS JAYME, O.F.M.

San Diego, October 17,

1772

———————— • ——————————

Translated and edited by

MAYNARD GEIGER, O.F.M.

Published for

THE SAN DIEGO PUBLIC LIBRARY

by Dawson's Book Shop, Los Angeles

1970

Contents

Introduction 9

Luís Jayme Letter 31

Facsimile of the
    Luís Jayme Letter 51

Introduction

THE possession of one of the few original letters of Fray Luís Jayme, O.F.M., by the San Diego Public Library, purchased from the Thomas Winthrop Streeter Collection, and the library's willingness to share its contents with the reading public come as no surprise to Californians who have just celebrated the bicentennial of the state's permanent European settlement and its introduction to Christianity. Jayme was one of California's rugged pioneers who happened to be placed in San Diego, which in its formative years might appropriately be called a disaster area.

It was at San Diego that the conquering Spaniards first set up housekeeping in the new land. There, because the conquest was a government enterprise, they had to conform with the "rule book" but because of unexpected situations they also had to "play it by ear." Added to this milieu were the diversities of characters in the principal agencies of conquest. Jayme was in the midst of the local situations and the personal conflicts. He

9

wrote as an eye-witness in a realistic way. What he noted in his revealing letter of October 17, 1772, the subject of this volume, does not make pleasant reading. He gives the details of a human struggle on the frontier where things were just getting started. California's bicentennial story is one from the stone age to the space age. Never was the situation more difficult than in the first decades of her history. It almost ceased to be a beginning and when near-disaster was overcome, its continued existence was often tenuous and the prospects frightening.

Fray Luís Jayme, California's proto-martyr, was, like Fray Junípero Serra, a native of Mallorca, the classic Mediterranean island that sent sixteen out of the 142 missionaries who evangelized California, the majority of whom were men of ability. Three of them became presidents of the missions. Jayme was born in the farming town of San Juan, just six miles southwest of Petra, the natal town of Serra, October 18, 1740, twenty-seven years after the birth of California's mission founder. At home he was known as Melchor Jaume (pronounced Djaume in the Mallorcan dialect). He was named after his father, his mother's maiden name being Margarita Vallespir. He attended the primary school of San Bernardino in Petra, the same school Serra had attended earlier. He entered the Franciscan order in Palma, the island's capital, September 27, 1760, just short of his twentieth birthday. After making his profession the following year and after the usual studies in philosophy and theology he was ordained a priest on December 22, 1764. From 1765 until 1770 he taught philosophy at the great Convento de San Francisco in Palma. From the chronological viewpoint, Jayme could hardly have been acquainted with Serra in Mallorca, for the latter had already left for America in 1749.

Jayme volunteered for the Indian missions of California the same year he arrived in Mexico as a member of the College of San Fernando. On January 20, 1771, he embarked on the *San Antonio* at San Blas together with nine other missionaries. The ship arrived at San Diego March 12 but sailed on to Monterey, where it anchored on May 21. There Serra welcomed the newcomers with open arms. Now the establishment of new missions could take place. Only those of San Diego and San Carlos had been founded. Serra soon assigned the new missionaries, sending Jayme and another Mallorcan, Fray Francisco Dumetz, to San Diego. The *San Antonio* bore the missionaries destined for the southern missions

together with Don Pedro Fages, regional commander, to San Diego, where they arrived on
July 14, just two years after the original Portolá
expedition had set out from the southern port in
search for Monterey, two days before the founding of the first mission by Serra. For Jayme, San
Diego was to be home until the tragic night of
November 5, 1775, when he was pierced by arrows and clubbed to death by the local Indians,
who had determined to wipe out the entire Spanish settlements, friars, soldiers, and civilians.[1]

Much may be gleaned from the extant letters
and reports emanating from California and Mexico between the years 1769 and 1775 concerning the complex state of affairs in the Spanish system of conquest. There were the surprised, un-
sophisticated Indians on the one hand and the
State-Church unity in conquest, a system devised
shortly after the effective discovery of America,
known as the *patronato real*, within whose
framework the king and his subaltern rulers dom-
inated church affairs in practically all externals.
Thus the missionaries became emissaries of the
Church as well as agents of the State. They had
to labor within that framework or not labor at

[1] See also Maynard Geiger, O.F.M., *Franciscan Missionaries in Hispanic
California 1769-1848. A Biographical Dictionary* (San Marino, 1969),
128-129.

all. The conquest of California consisted of civil, military, naval, religious, and economic elements. In agreement between José de Gálvez and Junípero Serra, in Lower California, the mission system to be introduced into California was to be based on the tried system in vogue in Texas and the Sierra Gorda. Financially the king's exchequer provided for the transportation of the missionaries and their belongings from Spain to Mexico. The Pious Fund—which the government had taken over from the Jesuits upon their expulsion in 1767—provided for the establishment of new missions and the maintenance of the missionaries.

Spain's initial purpose in coming to California was not a religious one. The conquest was politically motivated, chiefly for the containment of Russia. But as soon as the conquest became effective, Spain sincerely wished the mission system to become operative for the Christianization and civilization of the natives on the Spanish pattern. As in other areas of the Indies the missions were governed on a three-level basis: in the regional area, control was exercised between the military commander or governor and the president of the missions; in the middle area, between the viceroy and the ruling body of the College of San Fernando in Mexico; and finally at the highest level, between the king and Council of the Indies and the Franciscan commissary general in Madrid. There was also in San Diego the very local relationship between the natives, the presidio, and the mission. All these relationships were closely intertwined.

The Franciscans of the College of San Fernando were in charge of the Lower California missions from April 3, 1768, until April 14, 1772, when the Dominicans, their successors, arrived, though the formal transfer of the missions occurred sometime thereafter. The Franciscans had taken over fifteen ex-Jesuit missions and founded San Fernando de Velicatá on May 14, 1769, establishing San Diego on the following July 16. Palóu, the ex-president of the Lower California missions, arrived overland at San Diego with his companions on March 30, 1773. The gap between Velicatá and San Diego was a terrain of over 300 miles and this area was filled with seven missions by the Dominicans between 1774 and 1797. At a line about fifteen leagues south of San Diego Palóu marked the division line between the two mission territories with a cross and an appropriate inscription.

It was from Lower California that two overland expeditions under Rivera y Moncada and Portolá had come to found San Diego. It was to Lower California that Rivera returned early in 1770 to obtain supplies, and thither also went Fathers Dumetz and Cambón for the same reason in 1772. Cattle droves and mail carriers continued to use the Lower California trails to reinforce the new mission area and to keep up communications. In this early period the mission field of Upper California was referred to as "the new establishments of San Diego and Monterey." The governor of both Californias resided at Loreto in Lower California until 1777, when Felipe de Neve became the first resident governor at Monterey.

The three known letters of Fray Luís Jayme, all written in San Diego during his five years of tenure there, reveal a number of detailed, concrete facts concerning the mission system in its early days. Jayme's statements in these letters are amply corroborated in other contemporary ones such as those by Serra, Fages, Palóu, Crespí and Ortega. Jayme's first letter was written to Fray Francisco Palóu, then still in Lower California, August 22, 1772; the latter forwarded it to the College of San Fernando and today it is found in the files of the Mexican War Department. The second letter was directed to Fray Rafael Verger, O.F.M., guardian of the College of San Fernando, also a Mallorcan; it was written on October 17, 1772, the very day Serra boarded the *San Antonio* in San Diego harbor, and Jayme undoubtedly entrusted it to Serra personally to bring to the notice of Verger. It is this letter which is the subject of this monograph. The third Jayme letter was addressed to Serra while he was in Mexico, on April 3, 1773, and he received it before returning to California. Serra gave this letter to Verger, who in turn gave its contents to the viceroy, Antonio María Bucareli y Ursúa. It treated of the removal of Mission San Diego from Presidio Hill to Mission Valley. The Santa Barbara Mission Archive-Library has a transcript of this letter sent to Father Zephyrin Engelhardt, O.F.M., by Dr. Herbert E. Bolton early in this century on the letter head of Museo Nacional, Mexico City, stating it was copied from a certain Volume II, Lancaster-Jones Collection, of that institution. It was from this copy that Engelhardt produced his translation in his *San Diego Mission* (San Francisco, 1920), pp. 54-56. The present writer also has a photographic copy of the original from the Academy of American Franciscan History in Washington, D.C.

The first letter in part alludes to the subject of military immorality which is significantly treated in Jayme's second letter, where he also deals with economic and transportation problems together with unhappy relationships with Fages. The third deals mainly with the removal of the mission, agriculture, and a veiled reference to the unwholesome moral situation at San Diego. The mission site was effectively changed in August, 1774. At the same time the military encampment became a formal presidio. It was at this new site that Jayme met his fateful death in November of the following year.

The San Diego Indians of Yuman stock were troublesome to the soldiers and missionaries from the very beginning. They molested the sick and dying sailors at the improvised hospital along the bay. They were thievish in inclination especially with regard to cloth. What may be bluntly stated is that they did not like the Spanish presence in their midst. The gentle Fray Juan Crespí stated that "their avidity in stealing is unequalled." Miguel Costansó, the engineer, declared that "their greediness to rob can only be restrained by superior power and authority." José Francisco Ortega, scout of the Portolá expedition, wrote that they were "intrepid and haughty and very avaricious."[2] Serra felt frustrated when he failed in his first attempt to baptize an Indian baby.

San Diego and with it the entire California was almost abandoned when the *San Antonio*, which had been sent back to Mexico for a fresh crew of sailors and supplies, failed to appear before March 19, 1770. Meanwhile, the original mission site was attacked by the Indians on August 15, 1769, resulting in several deaths and some injuries on both sides. A beginning of conversions was made after Serra left for Monterey in April, 1770. However the registers of baptisms, marriages, and deaths, together with the *padrón* (family register), were burned in the conflagration of 1775. It was only in 1776 that Serra, together with Jayme's surviving fellow missionary, Fray Vicente Fuster, tried to put together from memory some of the lost details. Jayme in his letter of October 17, 1772, states that up to that time only fifty-five Indians, infants and adults, had been baptized and that he had desisted from baptizing four months prior to that because he could not sustain economically any more converts. Serra and Fuster could recall the names of only sixteen

[2] Geiger, *The Life and Times of Junipero Serra* (Washington, D.C., 1959), II, 230.

Indians who had been baptized in San Diego before the arrival of Jayme. Serra in the new register states that a total of 116 Indians had been baptized when he received the last report from
Jayme at the end of December, 1774. Fuster re-
membered that a total of 480 had been baptized
before November 5, 1775, more than 100 of
these in the month prior to the mission's destruction.[3] Thus Jayme's missionary work was pro-
gressing when the fatal blow came.

With regard to the policy of the missionaries
in not accepting more converts than they could
maintain in food and clothing, a practice followed
later also at Missions San Francisco and San Juan
Capistrano, they considered it essential that from
the beginning the newly baptized Indians should
learn to lead a regular Christian community life
at a mission rather than spending most of their
time away from the mission in search of food and
intermingling too much with the pagan Indians.
Or as Jayme put it, he preferred the Indians to remain good "pagans" rather than be "bad Christians." Still San Diego, which for many years remained one of the poorer missions economically,
had to tolerate what was often the case in Lower

[3] Data from "Libro Primero en que se asientan las partidas de las Bautis-
mos de esta Nueva Mision de San Diego" in the hand of Serra, September 16, 1776. Mission San Diego.

California, the absence of Indians from the mission because of limited agricultural return. Still a start had to be made. Jayme's ministry at San Diego was a difficult one. Yet some progress was made. When Palóu arrived at San Diego from Lower California, August 30, 1773, he could write: "There are now baptized, among children and adults, eighty-three. . . . They live in the village formed of their little houses of poles and tule, and near them live also the heathen catechumens, who punctually attend catechism every day. The heathen of the other villages also frequent the mission and attend catechism, being attracted by their delight in hearing the neophytes sing."[4] After Jayme's death Serra declared that the proto-martyr had learned the native language.

Palóu, less than a year after Jayme wrote his letter to Verger, gave a detailed description of Mission San Diego which indicates the progress made under Jayme's supervision. The mission church was still a log-cabin type with a tule roof but a beginning was being made for a new church of adobe with stone foundations. The missionaries' quarters were of adobe and wood with a tule roof. There was a warehouse for safeguard-

4 Herbert Eugene Bolton (tr.), *Historical Memoirs of New California by Fray Francisco Palóu, O.F.M.* (Berkeley, 1926), III, 215.

ing provisions. The neophytes had been engaged in the work, but building had to be halted temporarily because of lack of food, which again the converted Indians had to seek in the open country. Cattle and other animals had increased. Agricultural implements were on hand but produce was poor. Exploration had been made over a radius of ten leagues for a more suitable place for the mission but running water could not be found. Pasture for cattle was abundant.[5]

The reason for the presence of Serra and Fages in San Diego late in 1772 when Jayme was in charge of the mission was the arrival of the ships *San Antonio* and *San Carlos* laden with supplies for the missions and presidios. Because of unfavorable winds they could proceed no farther north than the Santa Barbara Islands with the result that they anchored in the southern bay. Monterey was notified by overland courier. Fages and Serra would have to come south for their supplies and have them hauled as far north as Monterey.[6] Leaving there with a military escort on August 24, 1772, they founded Mission San Luis Obispo on September 1, and arrived at San Diego

[5] *Ibid.*, 214-217.
[6] On arrival at San Diego, Serra persuaded Juan Pérez to attempt the voyage north nevertheless, which he successfully accomplished. He was captain of the *San Antonio*.

on September 16. Between then and October 17, when Serra boarded the vessel bound for Mexico, he experienced a troublous period. There is no indication that Serra had intended going to Mexico when he left Monterey. However, after his accumulated dissatisfactions in the north to which were added new asperities at San Diego, after conferences with Jayme and three other missionaries who urged him to make the journey, he decided to go. His purpose was to lay before the viceroy the troubled California situation and to appeal to him to institute appropriate legislation to remedy affairs.

Captain Pedro Fages, commander of the Catalonian volunteers, had come from Spain a few years before and served for a brief period in Sonora. He had come as a lieutenant and had been raised to the captaincy during his early career in California. An undeveloped mission field was something new to him and his soldiers. Fages was a strict disciplinarian, if not something of a martinet, who succeeded in alienating many of the soldiers as well as the missionaries. There had been frequent bickerings between Fages and Serra in the Carmel-Monterey area and their relationship at San Diego was anything but pleasant. Soldiers had twice deserted at San Diego and were brought back only through the influence of Fathers Paterna and Dumetz. In the north a number had become discontented. A few wrote to Serra to use his influence to have them sent home. Fages was accused on more than one occasion of not keeping his plighted word. In Mexico, Bucareli, new in his office, was worried and perplexed over the situation in California because of the disharmony between the religious and military arms of the conquest and wrote a number of letters concerning it both to California and to Spain. He actually feared that the conquest would fail because of it.

Various questions arose in San Diego with regard to the economic and transportation matters which Jayme treats of in his letter to Verger. Serra verbally and in writing to Fages at this time deals with similar matters. Fages complained about the fifty-five baptized Indians who could not be adequately fed at the mission and, as Jayme points out, he was niggardly about providing for the Indian instructors from Lower California and refused to provide for the baptized or heathen Indians. According to Serra, Fages wanted the Christian Indian village removed to another place for which, the president asserted, he gave ridiculous reasons. Fages used mission mules for haul-

ing water to the ships in the harbor and for trans-
porting presidio materials to land, tiring out the
mission mules and thus preventing their use by
the padres. Mission San Gabriel was in dire straits
and mission mules were needed to transport articles there before the beginning of the rainy sea-
son. Serra had to ask Fages just what the obliga-
tions of the soldiers were with regard to building
when a mission was being founded and got a definite reply. The missionaries disliked the appor-
tioning of food to the soldiers since this brought
about some complaints from the military. Fages
discontinued this practice, but reluctantly, stating that since the missionaries did not want to
perform this act of "charity" he consented.
Amidst all this lack of agreement Fages quoted
to Serra a letter wherein Bucareli had written to
the commander urging Serra and his missionaries
to obey him. Nor would Fages show the letter to
Serra upon his request for the president could not
imagine on what evidence he had given such an
order.[7] Fages himself had received more than one
letter urging him to work in harmony with the
missionaries and once Bucareli stated that in a

[7] Facsimiles of these letters together with their translations with intro-
ductory remarks were published in a limited edition by the Grabhorn
Press, San Francisco, December 23, 1936, under the title: *Fages-Serra
Letters A.D. MDCCLXXII.*

new country like California matters could not be handled as in a firmly established area.

Finally, there occurred at San Diego a heated altercation between Fages and José de Cañizares, captain and second pilot of the *San Antonio*, over the former's delay in delivering the mail to be taken to Mexico. This became a shouting match which Fages considered serious enough to recount to Bucareli in detail.[8] All of these facts taken together prove that San Diego was not too pleasant a place in September and October of 1772 and that details on the mission system had to be worked out better among the agencies of conquest; for that very reason Serra went to Mexico in person. Jayme lived in the midst of these unpleasant occurrences and it was in this milieu that his letter was written.

One final matter, a most serious one, still has to be considered. One of the unpleasant difficulties that confronted the missionaries was the immorality of a number of the soldiers. If the missionaries were to convert the Indians from paganism to Christianity and to convince them of the latter's superiority, preaching had to be reinforced by example. The latter part of Jayme's let-

[8] Sections of the heated quarrel are given in Geiger, *Life and Times*, I, 335-336.

ter of October 17, 1772, deals with this problem in great detail. From the very beginning of the conquest there were breaches in the moral code, a matter that continued for long after. Soldiers were necessary for protection and for certain services in building, in acting as majordomos, for carrying the mail, and for accompanying droves of animals. Many were illiterate, uneducated, but still they were Christians. It was difficult for Indians to understand how, if Christian morality was based on Christian belief, Christian soldiers who held those beliefs could disregard the consequent code of morals. Jayme brings out their reasoning very well. Still only Spaniards were called by themselves as *gente de razón*, the inference being that Indians were without reasoning powers. The Indians without the knowledge of Christian faith had a certain moral code whose infringement they punished, a realization that brought tears to Jayme's eyes. He was placed in an unanswerable position.

When Gálvez gave instructions to Portolá at Cape San Lucas, February 20, 1769, on how the conquest was to be conducted, among other things he declared that he, Portolá, "shall point out to them [the soldiers] as an inviolable regulation the need for treating the Indians well and he shall punish them as for an irremissable crime any molestations or violence toward the native women for, besides being offenses against God which they would commit by such excesses, they could also endanger the success of the expedition."[9] Still we know from the testimony of Fray Pedro Font, O.F.M., chronicler of the Anza expedition in 1776, that when the expedition passed through the Santa Barbara Channel lands, the Indian women hid themselves wondering if a certain Camacho who had committed outrages during an earlier period, was among the group.[10] The notorious scandals committed by the soldiers shortly after the founding of Mission San Gabriel are recorded in detail by Serra, Palóu, and the resident padres.[11] Similar offenses were commited at Mission San Antonio, where soldiers violated the wives of Indians in the latters' very presence.

In Serra's letter to Bucareli, April 22, 1773, dealing with the retention of the port of San Blas as a point of embarcation for men and material for the California missions and presidios as against

9 This original document is in the Archivo General de Indias, Seville. A translation by Geiger may be found in the *Southern California Quarterly* (Los Angeles, Calif.), June, 1965. The citation is found on p. 212.
10 Bolton (tr.), *Anza's California Expeditions* (Berkeley, 1930), IV, 252.
11 Cf. Zephyrin Engelhardt, O.F.M., *San Gabriel Mission* (San Gabriel, Calif., 1927), 3-16, and Geiger, *Life and Times*, I, 303-308.

a plan for overland transportation among other things, he wrote: "the third point . . . needs no more proof than is provided each day by the soldiers who without any fear of God whatever in their hearts, give such scandal in those far distant parts. Your Excellency has been fully informed about it. . . . Then too the presence of so many women there [along the road of travel]—it would be a great miracle, yes a whole series of miracles, if it did not provoke so many men of such low character to disorders which we have to lament in all our missions; they occur every day; it is as though a plague of immorality has broken out. I have seen it myself, and, in the bitterness of their hearts, the religious missionaries have written to me about it in their recent letters. But the subject is so distasteful that I do not want to linger on it to any further extent."[12]

Fages himself in a letter to Bucareli on June 2, 1773, acknowledged that two soldiers had attacked two young pagan girls and that one had died. These soldiers were imprisoned and later were sent to San Blas for further adjudication.

It was for good reasons that Serra in his famous *representación* of March 13, 1773, requested

---

[12] The original is in the Santa Barbara Mission Archive-Library. Printed and translated in Antonine Tibesar, O.F.M., *Writings of Junípero Serra* (Washington, D.C., 1955) I, 331-343. The citation is found on pp. 339-341.

from the viceroy the right of the missionaries to request from Fages' successor removal from any mission of a soldier accused by a missionary of immoral behavior, to be replaced by one of better conduct. This request was granted. Despite the passage of such appropriate legislation, moral offenses continued to occur. When Serra called Felipe de Neve's attention to these continued affronts and was answered in a supercilious way, the president wrote in confidence to his trusted minister at San Diego, Fray Fermín Francisco de Lasuen; "He allows fornication among the soldiers—so I have heard him say from his own mouth—it is winked at in Rome and tolerated in Madrid. But fornication is an offense against the law of God and spells damnation of souls."[13]

In my *Life and Times of Fray Junípero Serra*, I stated on the basis of the brief statement of Jayme to Palóu anent military immorality: "While I do not wish to overstress such incidents as the immediate cause of the San Diego revolt one can hardly deny that Indian resentment against such abuses must have been great." On reading Jayme's more explicit letter of October 17, I am more inclined to state that military immorality must have been a contributing factor. In

[13] Geiger, *Life and Times*, II, 60.

that case Jayme was the innocent victim of his own *gente de razón*. It was that body of degraded men who prepared the way for the prevalence in mission California of the *mal gálico* which already by 1812 was decimating the natives and which, in my opinion, more than any other cause, destroyed their numbers.

Somewhere within the mission church of San Diego lie the mortal remains of Fray Luís Jayme. In the arroyo nearby is a concrete cross recalling the area where his bludgeoned and pierced body was found on the morning of November 6, 1775. In distant San Juan in Mallorca a monument to him stands above the town hall. In the sacristy of the local church is a painting of his savage martyrdom. Jayme lives in the affections of his latter-day Californians as the noble pioneer who gave his life in his endeavor to plant in this land the principles of Christianity. An original letter of his, one of San Diego's "incunabula" documents, after 198 years has come back to rest close to where it was written in days of stress and uncertainty.

Long live Jesus, Mary, and Joseph.
The Very Reverend Father Guardian,
Raphael Verger: The grace of the
Holy Spirit be with Your Reverence and
with me. Amen.

O N July 30, there arrived at this port of San Diego His Majesty's ship called *El Príncipe*,[14] and on the 13th day of August there arrived another ship, the *San Carlos*,[15] both of which came here because they were unable to reach the port of Monterey. On September 16 there arrived from Monterey Father President Junípero Serra and Captain Pedro Fages, and, although the vessels brought eight hundred *fanegas*[16] of corn, Fages would not give this mission more than one-half of half a *cuartillo*[17] of corn

---

[14] Alias the *San Antonio.*   [15] Alias *El Toysón.*
[16] A *fanega* is equal to about 1.6 bushels. John N. Bowman, "Weights and Measures in Provincial California," *California Historical Society Quarterly*, XXX, No. 4, p. 315. Manuel Carrera Stampa in "The Evolution of Weights and Measures in New Spain," translated by Robert S. Smith, *The Hispanic American Historical Review*, (Chapel Hill, N. Carolina) XXIX, 14-15, gives the *fanega* the equivalent of 2.58 U.S. bushels. See also his discussion on variants, *ibid.*, 318-323.
[17] A *cuartillo*, usually a liquid measure, was .12 of a gallon. "It was originally intended to be the equivalent in weight of one pound." As an arid measure, however, a *cuartillo* was equal to 1.72 dry quarts. Stampa, *op. cit.*, 14-15.

for the Indians from the Californias,[18] which is just enough for one meal despite the fact they have no other provisions. For the local Christian natives and for the gentiles, he would not give anything. Thus the Californians,[19] granting that they know how to work a little, will have small chance to do so because they will have very little to eat, and there is no place to look for food. We cannot make the natives around here work, and often we cannot teach them the doctrine because they have to go hunting for food every day. Fifty-five have been baptized, counting both children and adults, and, although on the one hand I am happy that we have converted [some of] the heathen, on the other hand it grieves me sorely to see that for lack of food we shall not be able to teach them everything that is necessary.

What grieves me most is that two interpreters,[20] who were among the first that were bap-

18 Jayme's reference is to Lower or Baja California. Usually the use of the plural refers to Upper and Lower California.

19 Here again the reference is to the Lower California Christian Indians who came along with the Rivera and Portolá expeditions.

20 One of these interpreters was no doubt Diego Rivera, mentioned by Jayme later in his letter, and who is noted in the Baptismal Register of Mission San Diego, newly fashioned by Serra after the conflagration of November 5, 1775, in which the originals were burned. On September 23, 1776, Serra states that Rivera had been baptized by Fray Francisco Gomez, at about the age of eighteen, was given the name Diego but that in 1776 he was known as Miguel. Fernando de Rivera y Moncada was his godfather. Serra adds: "He was a very useful interpreter but today (1776) he is one of the prisoners for having been an accomplice in the revolt [of November, 1775]."

tized and already knew something of the Spanish language, now are forgetting what little they did know, and we have no others whom we could use, either to learn the language or to teach the Christians and gentiles. These interpreters can rarely come to the mission because they have to go out and gather their seeds. For about four months now we have not baptized a single one, and I, for one, do not intend to baptize any more unless other measures are taken, for it is better for them to be gentiles than bad Christians.

The captain wants and has requested families from the other side[21] to work for and advance the missions, and I, in reality, do not understand it, for, supposing that there are in the missions some Indians from the Californias, these, and among them most of the new Christians, could work as much or more than the families[22] that can come, yet he will not give them anything to eat, saying that Indians will not be fed, and that no rations whatever shall be given to them. Therefore, if instructions are not issued saying that the Indians shall be fed, and what amount is to be given to each mission, not leaving it to the discretion of this gentleman here, we shall always remain at the beginning and never advance at all. The lands

[21] From Lower California or from the mainland of Mexico.
[22] He is referring to agricultural workers other than Indians.

of this mission are so good that a little wheat which was planted yielded very well without irrigation, and some four or five *fanegas* have been harvested.[23] The only thing lacking is corn to support the Indians so that they can work, although it would not be bad if there were some Europeans here[24] so that they could work and teach others to do so.

Last year Captain Pedro Fages gave eight pack mules, two saddle mules, and two horses for the founding of this mission. Father Dumetz[25] brought some mules from the Californias, but the said gentleman is using everything, ordering that everything in the ship be unloaded on these few overburdened mules as if they were his own. Furthermore, if this continues we shall not have any mules in less than two years. We cannot use them to haul wood and plant our crops at least to some

[23] Palóu states when writing in 1773 that in the first year of the mission's existence the water of the San Diego River rose so high that it carried away the planted seeds and in the subsequent year which was a dry one the seed was lost because of a lack of water. Bolton, *Historical Memoirs*, III, 216. Those plantings had been made near the mission site. However, wheat was then planted about two leagues away from the mission, where rain fell more heavily. It was probably to this newly chosen area that Jayme refers when describing the land as "good."

[24] Compare with note 22.

[25] Dumetz and Fray Pedro Benito Cambón, the latter from Mission San Gabriel, had been sent to Lower California to obtain supplies in order to stave off hunger at Missions San Diego and San Gabriel. Dumetz returned to San Diego and among other things brought perhaps the first sheep into Upper California. Engelhardt, *Mission San Diego*, 42-43.

extent; so everything is lost. Thus if the mules
and horses which he gave, and those which they
brought from the Californias are to be used according to the wishes of this man, and if the mission is to use them very little, or none at all, it
would be better if the former had never been received and the latter had not been brought from
the Californias. Last year after the mules had been
given to the missions, he had more than a hundred
mules left, and now when he came with the Father President to carry off the provisions, he
brought just a few for the escorts, and nearly half
of these belonged to the missions. When I told
him that he had brought very few mules to haul
away the said provisions, he replied that it would
be made up of mules belonging to the mission, for
they all belonged to the king. So it is that we cannot plow at the missions because the mules are
being used for the king's business. Consequently,
we cannot do any planting, and likewise, since he
did not bring enough mules, they are going hun-
gry at Mission San Gabriel, even after the arrival
of two vessels. It is about a league and a half from
this mission to the landing, and already from hauling water from here to the ships and from hauling
the king's provisions (which should have been
hauled by the king's mules) the mules have

reached such a state that most of them are played out and weak from not eating, for they scarcely have time to rest. They can no longer carry an entire load because they fall down on the road. Consequently these kinds of gifts which have been made to the missions, as I see it, are just gifts in name and not in fact. Twenty-five animals had been given to this mission, and Don Pedro took away those that he wanted, and, as I see it, gave, as a matter of form only, eight pack mules, two saddle mules, and two horses. I am not telling you about how it happened, for I suppose that Your Reverence already knows. Moreover, Father President Junipero Serra is already writing you about it.[26]

As for working, I wish to tell you that last year a little wheat was planted, the work being done by a leather-jacket soldier. He and a brother of his had offered to work for the mission, but Don Pedro heard of it and took them away from here. This gentleman tells them before the fathers that they are to work for the mission, but by his deeds he tells them the contrary. From the month of

[26] This was not the last controversy about mules. In 1775 Rivera appropriated mules that had been sent for the missions and told Serra in a letter: "Believe me, Your Reverence, in order that Missions can exist, there must be presidios and there are no presidios when soldiers are going about on foot." Geiger, *Life and Times*, II, 22. In 1772 Fages took a similar view, stressing need in the concrete circumstances even if the needs of the mission had to be overlooked.

March until the vessels arrived, two Indians and I worked on a chest in which we could put the supplies, and this gentleman as soon as he arrived from Monterey took a fancy to it, and, although he was offered another in which to place his things, which, although it was not as good, with the people he had he could have repaired it in four days and used it, but he did not want to, saying that he would throw all the supplies in the middle of the plaza. In order to prevent such a silly thing from being done, I lent him the new chest.[27] To all new missions, if there are only gentiles and these do not know how to work, there should be given a muleteer to manage the mules, a cowboy, and some people to work in the field and teach the new Christians to work, but at none of these have we been given anything but one muleteer, and Don Pedro takes him away whenever the notion strikes him, and we have been left without a muleteer, cowboy, or anything else that would serve to advance the mission. Consequently, it is necessary for the fathers to be versed in the general art of Blessed Raymond;[28] otherwise we should be left without anything.

[27] Fages is here described in characteristic fashion as arbitrary and demanding.
[28] Reference is to Blessed Ramón Lull of Mallorca, considered the island's

With reference to the Indians, I wish to say that great progress would be made if there was anything to eat and the soldiers would set a good example. We cannot give them anything to eat because what Don Pedro has given is not enough to last half a year for the Indians from the Californias who are here. Thus little progress will be made under present conditions. As for the example to be set by the soldiers, no doubt some of them are good exemplars and deserve to be treated accordingly, but very many of them deserve to be hanged on account of the continuous outrages which they are committing in seizing and raping the women. There is not a single mission where all the gentiles have not been scandalized, and even on the roads, so I have been told. Surely, as the gentiles themselves state, they are committing a thousand evils, particularly those of a sexual na-

---

outstanding man and hero. (b.c. 1235 in Palma, d. 1316 probably in Tunis as a martyr.) After a worldly life he converted to one of asceticism and turned his talents to philosophy, mysticism, and the study of Oriental languages. Among other things he wrote the *Art.* "The Art could work on all levels of creation, the angelic world, the world of the stars, of man and his activities, of the animal and vegetable worlds," etc. See the *New Catholic Encyclopedia* under Lull, VIII, pp. 1074-1075. It is clear what Jayme intended to say, that the missionaries were expected to be jacks of all trades from whom was expected universal knowledge and varied skills owing to the way things were being handled in California. Verger, as a fellow Mallorcan, would clearly understand Jayme's meaning. Mallorca's university at Palma, where Serra had been a professor, was named after Ramón or Raymundo Lulio.

ture. The fathers have petitioned Don Pedro concerning these points, but he has paid very little
attention to them. He has punished some, but as
soon as they promised him that they would work
at the presidio, he turned them loose. That is what
he did last year, but now he does not even punish
them or say anything to them on this point. I suppose that some ministers will write you, each concerning his own mission, and therefore I shall not
tell you about the cases which have occurred at
other missions. I shall speak only of Mission San
Diego.

At one of these Indian villages near this mission of San Diego, which said village is very large,
and which is on the road that goes to Monterey,[29]
the gentiles therein many times have been on the
point of coming here to kill us all, and the reason
for this is that some soldiers went there and raped
their women, and other soldiers who were carrying the mail to Monterey turned their animals

[29] No doubt this was the village named by Crespí as the "Village of the
Springs of the Rinconada de San Diego," which he described as about
two leagues from the original mission site and which was "a very large
village of heathen who are in a valley formed by this second harbor"
(False Bay). And it was on the road to Monterey. Bolton (tr.), *Fray
Juan Crespí Missionary Explorer of the Pacific Coast* (Berkeley, 1927),
122-123. Palóu places El Rincón about half a league from the mission
on the road to Monterey. Bolton, *Historical Memoirs*, I, 309. Fernando
Rivera y Moncada states that El Rincón was located along the "second
bay nearby which is within sight." Ernest J. Burrus, S.J. (ed.), *Diaro
del Capitan Comandante Fernando de Rivera y Moncada* (Madrid,
1967), I, 228.

into their fields and they ate up their crops. Three other Indian villages about a league or a league and a half from here[30] have reported the same thing to me several times. For this reason on several occasions when Father Francisco Dumetz or I have gone to see these Indian villages, as soon as they saw us they fled from their villages and fled to the woods or other remote places, and the only ones who remained in the village were some men and some very old women. The Christians here have told me that many of the gentiles of the aforesaid villages leave their huts and the crops which they gather from the lands around their villages, and go to the woods and experience hunger. They do this so that the soldiers will not rape their women as they have already done so many times in the past.

No wonder the Indians here were bad when the mission was first founded. To begin with, they did not know why they [the Spaniards] had come, unless they intended to take their lands away from them. Now they all want to be Christians because they know that there is a God who created the heavens and earth and all things, that there is a Hell, and Glory, that they have souls, etc., but when the mission was first founded they

[30] These villages are difficult to identify since Jayme does not indicate in what direction they lay.

did not know all these things; instead, they thought they were like animals, and when the vessels came at first, they saw that most of the crews died; they were very loathe to pray, and they did not want to be Christians at all; instead, they said that it was bad to become a Christian and then they would die immediately. No wonder they said so when they saw how most of the sailors and California Indians died, but now, thanks be to the Lord, God has converted them from Sauls to Pauls.[31] They all know the natural law, which, so I am informed, they have observed as well or better than many Christians elsewhere. They do not have any idols; they do not go on drinking sprees; they do not marry relatives; and they have but one wife. The married men sleep with their wives only. The bachelors sleep together, and apart from the women and married couples. If a man plays with any woman who is not his wife, he is scolded and punished by his captains. Concerning those from the Californias I have heard it said that they are given to sexual vices, but among those here I have not been able to discover a single fault of that nature. Some of the first adults whom we baptized, when we pointed out to them that it was wrong to have

[31] Reference is to the conversion of St. Paul as recorded in the *Acts of the Apostles*. Paul was named Saul before his conversion.

sexual intercourse with a woman to whom they
were not married, told me that they already knew
that, and that among them it was considered to
be very bad, and so they did not do so at all. "The
soldiers," they told me, "are Christians and, although they know that God will punish them in
Hell, do so, having sexual intercourse with our
wives. We," they said, "although we did not
know that God would punish us for that in Hell,
considered it to be very bad, and we did not do it,
and even less now that we know that God will
punish us if we do so." When I heard this, I burst
into tears to see how these gentiles were setting
an example for us Christians. Of the many cases
which have occurred in this mission, I shall tell
of only two, about which it is very necessary that
Your Reverence should know, particularly the
last one which I shall relate.

[First Case]

ONE day about the first of August of the
present year of 1772, I went to the Indian village nearest the mission, which is
about fifty paces from here,[32] and the Christian

---

[32] Cosoy, the aboriginal San Diego Indian settlement. Palóu states that
"both the beach and the vicinity of the mission are very well populated
with heathen, and in the district of about ten leagues there are more
than twenty large villages, one of them being close to the mission."
Bolton, *Historical Memoir*, III, 214.

Indians said to me: "Father, there is an unmarried woman here who is pregnant." "Well, how can this be?" I said to them. "Have not you told me many times that you do not have sexual intercourse with any woman except your own wife?" "That is true, Father," they said to me. "We do not do so, nor have any of us done so with this woman. On the contrary, according to what the woman says, she was coming from the Rincón village (which is about a league and a half[33] from this mission) when a soldier named Hernandez[34] and a soldier named Bravo[35] and a soldier named Julian Murillo seized her and sinned with her, and, although she was getting away, she is almost blind and could not run very fast, and so it is that she is in this condition without being married." They told me, furthermore, that she was ashamed to be in this condition without being married, and that for this reason she had made many attempts to have an abortion but could not, but that as soon as the creature was born she would kill it. I told her through the interpreter (for, although I understood her some, I used the interpreter so that she could understand better) that she should

---

[33] A little over three miles away. See note 29.

[34] His full name was José Rafael Hernández. See H. H. Bancroft, *History of California* (San Francisco, 1886), I, 737.

[35] His full name was José Marcelino Bravo. *Ibid.*, I, 734.

not do anything so foolish, for God would punish her in Hell, that she should bear the little one and we would give her clothing for it to wear, and we would baptize it, etc. Several times I made this and other exhortations to her so that she would not carry out her evil intentions, but it was to no avail. When the time came for the child to be born, she went to the said Rincón village, where she bore the child and killed it, without my being able to baptize it. The child was killed about the middle of August of this year. The Indians who saw the little boy told me that he was somewhat white and gave every indication of being a son of the soldiers.

[Second Case]

On the 11th day of September of the present year there went to the Indian village called "El Corral"[36] the soldiers Castelo,[37]

[36] According to the official investigation of the San Diego uprising of 1775 conducted by José Francisco Ortega, El Corral was adjacent to a place called San Luis, which was located about three leagues or about eight and a quarter miles from the presidio. It was in the direction of the sierra, hence beyond the second location of the mission. *Dilixencias sobre el Alzamineto o sublebacion que el dia cinco de Novre. hubo a la una de la noche, en la Mission de Sn. Diego en el ano de 1775.* This original document is in the Doheny Memorial Library at St. John's Seminary, Camarillo, California. There is a photostat of the same in the Santa Barbara Mission Archive-Library. It is printed in Burrus,

Juan María Ruiz,[38] Bravo, and another who, although the Indians did not know his name, they knew his face well, and a sailor named Ignacio Marques. When they arrived at the said Indian village, they asked the Indian women for prickly pear apples, which they graciously gave to them. They then asked them to give them some earthen pots, and when they would not do so, the soldier Castelo went forward to take them by force in front of Marques, the said sailor, and boldly seized one of the women by the hand. The said sailor left the soldiers, giving them to understand that he did not want to cooperate in such iniquity as the soldiers were going to commit, and in fact did commit, as soon as the said sailor left them.

Before the said soldiers sinned with the women, the soldier Castelo and the soldier Bravo threatened a Christian Indian named José Antonio[39] who happened to be at the said Indian village, so that he would say nothing about what he

---

op. cit., I, 428-481. The Indians of El Corral participated in the destruction of the mission. Ortega mentions El Corral nine times between pp. 242 and 454. Burrus, op. cit.

[37] His full name was Agustín Castelo. Bancroft, op. cit., I, 734.

[38] Bancroft lists him also as being in California between 1769 and 1773. Op. cit., I, 737.

[39] He is listed in the San Diego Baptismal Register as having been baptized as an adult of about twenty years old and was from the village of El Corral. No date is given but the baptism occurred either in 1771 or 1772, during the ministry of Jayme.

had seen. Soldier Castelo carried a gentile woman into a corral which serves as a part of the en-
closure surrounding the said Indian village, and
inside the corral the said soldier had sexual intercourse with the woman and sinned with her.
When he had raped her, the said soldier came out
of the corral, and the soldier Juan María Ruiz
entered the same corral and sinned with the said
woman. After this they released the woman and
went to the Indian village, and the soldier whose
name is not known seized another woman vio-
lently and carried her into the same corral and
sinned with her there. He came out, and the soldier Bravo entered and sinned with her. He came
out and the soldier Juan María Ruiz entered and
did the same. He came out and the soldier Castelo
entered and did the same. They went to the Indian village and the soldier Castelo gave this last
woman two tortillas and some red ribbons. The
soldier Juan María Ruiz also gave this same woman some ribbons. The two said soldiers also gave
the first woman some ribbons. In order that these
outrages should not become known, soldiers Castelo and Bravo told José Antonio, the Indian
(who is the one already mentioned above, he
having been at the Indian village while all this was
taking place) that if he told the father they would

punish him. The said José Antonio arrived here at the mission and the soldier Castelo gave him two tortillas, warning him not to tell.

On the afternoon of the same day the two women came to tell me about what had happened. They came into the mission weeping, and were seen by many soldiers who were inside. Guessing why they had come, I sent them to the Indian village next to the mission so that the case would not become known to the public. I went to the Indian village after a little while and learned about everything that had happened from the same women with whom the said soldiers had sinned, Diego Ribera[40] serving as my interpreter for greater clarity, he being the one whom I use to teach the Christian Doctrine.

I was informed of this case twice by the said two women, and three times by José Antonio, the said Indian, and they always agreed on everything. This evil was followed by another which, *abisus abisum invocat*,[41] was: namely, that this

40 See note 20.
41 "Deep calls unto deep," found in Psalm (42) 43, verse 8. The new Latin translation of the Psalms authorized by Pope Pius XII renders the Latin: "Gurges gurgitem vocat." The English translation in *The Jerusalem Bible* renders the full verse in this fashion: "Deep is calling to deep as your cataracts roar; all your waves, your breakers have rolled over me." This Psalm was sung by the Jews during their captivity, expressing a longing for a return to their homeland and the misery experienced in exile. Jayme's reference is obvious in the circumstances in which he found himself.

same Indian who had told me about this case was placed in stocks without my being notified, and I took him out in defiance of the corporal of the guard, for I judged, and rightly so, that they were going to punish him so that he would not confess the truth concerning the said case. I am not writing you all the details of the case because Father President Junípero Serra has already written you all the details.[42] I beg Your Reverence to do everything possible (as I suppose you will) so that this conquest will not be lost or retarded because of the bad example of these soldiers, also so that it may be materially restored. In the memorial[43] I am asking for a little sun dial adjustable to any latitude, one like the one which Your Reverence had made for Father Antonio Paterna[44] when he was in the Sierra Gorda. I should appreciate it if Your Reverence would send for it or have it made. Enclosed you will find the memorial from the fathers at Mission San Luis Obispo,[45] which,

42 This letter has not come to light.
43 A memorial (Spanish, *memoria*) was a request in writing of the detailed articles needed by a definite mission.
44 Paterna came to California with Jayme. After Serra's departure for Mexico and until Palóu's arrival from Lower California (October 17, 1772—March 30, 1773) Paterna was acting president of the Upper California missions.
    Paterna had come to America shortly after Serra and was a missionary in the Sierra Gorda missions from 1750 to 1770, when the College of San Fernando relinquished those missions to the archbishop of Mexico. The Sierra Gorda missions were located in the northeastern area of the present state of Querétaro. The churches built during Serra's administration are still in use.
45 Father José Cavaller was in charge.

since they neglected to include it among their papers, they forwarded to me so that I could submit it to Your Reverence with mine.

I remain, Your Reverence, as ever, praying that God will watch over you and preserve you for many years in his divine love and grace. From this Mission of San Diego, October 17, 1772.

Kissing the hands of Your Reverence, always your most affectionate friend and faithful, humble subject.

FRIAR LUIS JAYME
[Rubric]

[Endorsed:] Friar Luís Jayme

[In another hand:]

THE Indians killed him, and on his knees he said to them before he died, among other things: "Children, love God!"[46] And one of the Indians, seizing a large stone, let it fall upon his head, saying: "No love God any more." Thus the said father ended his apostolic life.[47]

---

[46] The expression *"Amar a Dios"* was the usual greeting in early California, introduced into the land by the Franciscan missionaries.

[47] A graphic description of the San Diego massacre and conflagration in 1775 is given by Father Vicente Fuster, who sent the account to Serra, then in Monterey, November 28, 1775. Serra sent the document on to the College of San Fernando. The account is given in Spanish with English translation in Tibesar, *Writings of Junípero Serra*, II, 449-458. The description given here about the "large stone" was written by someone in Mexico; Jayme was pierced by arrows and beaten with clubs.

Facsimile of the
Luis Jayme Letter

Viva Jesus Maria y Joseph

M.R.P. Guardian Raphael Verger.

La gracia del Espiritu Santo sea con V.R. y conmigo
Amen.

Dia 30 de Julio llegò à este puerto de Sn Diego el Bar
co de su Magestad, llamado el Principe, y dia 13 de
Agosto llegò el otro Barco Sn Carlos, los quales por no
poder coger el puerto de Monterrey, vinieron acà. Dia
16 de Septiembre llegò de Monterrey el P. Presidente Junipero Serra, y el capitan Dn Pedro Fages, y aunque los
Barcos hayan traìdo 8 cientas fanegas de maiz, à esta

Cargo.
800 fanegas
de maiz.

La mitad de me=
dio quartillo de
maiz para los
Californios: para
los nuevos chris-
tianos nada.

mission no quiso dar mas que la mitad de medio quartillo
de maiz para los Indios de Californias, el qual no basta
mas que para una comida, porque no tienen otra cosa:
para los naturales de acà ya para los Christianitos, y ya
para los Gentiles nada quiso dar, y assi los de Californias
supuesto que saben trabajar algo, muy poco podràn por
tener una muy chica comida, ni hay en donde buscarla;
Los naturales de acà no los podemos hacer trabajar, y muchas veces enseñarles la doctrina, porque es preciso, que
ellos vayan à buscarla todos los dias su comida. 55
son los que se han bautizado entre parvulos, y Adultos,
y aunque de una parte estoy por haver salido del estado de Gentilidad, pero de otra parte me dà pena, y
desconsuelo ver que por falta de comida, no los podemos
enseñar todo lo preciso, y lo que mas me desconsuela es que
los interpretes, que fueron de los primeros que se bautizaron

Los quales ya sabian algo de la lengua castellana ahora van perdiendo lo poco que sabian, y no tenemos otros de quienes nos podamos servir, ya para aprehender la lengua, y ya para poder enseñar del todo los Chrixtianitos, y Gentiles. Estos interpretes solamente una tal qual vez puede venir à la Mission, porque es preciso que ellos vayan à coger su semilla. habrà como unos quatro meses que no hemos bautizado alguno, y yo de mi parte no ago cuenta de bautizar mas sino dan otras providencias, porque vale mas que sean Gentiles, que si despues de Christianos, han de ser malos. El Sr Capitan està deseando, y pidiendo familias de la otra banda paraque trabajen y adelanten las Missiones, y yo en realidad no lo entiendo por supuesto que en las missiones hay algunos Indios de californias que estos y entre estos los mas de Chrixtianos nuevos podian trabajar tanto o mas que las familias que pueden venir no les quiere dar de comer diciendo que los Indios no comen ni se les dà racion alguna, y assi sino viene determinado de que den de comer à los Indios, y que cantidad se haya de dar à cada mission, no dexandolo à la disposicion de este Cavallero de acà, nos estaremos siempre en los principios sin adelantamiento alguno. Las tierras de esta mission son buenas de suerte que un poco de trigo que se sembrò se dio de temporal muy bueno, y se hà cogido como unas quatro, o cinco fanegas. solamente lo que falta es maiz para mantener los Indios paraque puedan trabajar aunque no seria malo de que hubiera alguna

gente de razon paraque trabajaran, y enseñaran á
trabajar. El año pasado dió el Sr Capitan Dn Pedro fages
ocho mulas de carga, y dos de silla, y dos cavallos para la
fundación de essa, el P. Gumez trajo de californias algunas mulas, y de todo se sirve el dicho Cavallero man-
dando carrear todo lo del Barco con essas pocas y malas
mulas como si fueran suyas propias, y á mas de que siepo
va assi en menos de dos años ya no habrá mulas, no nos
podemos servir de ellas para carrear Leña, y arar un
poco para sembrar hechandolo á perder todo, y assi si
las mulas, y cavallos que dió, y las que trajeron de
californias han de servir por lo que el dicho Sr quisiere
y nada, o, muy poco se haya de servir de ellas la Mission
valiera mas ni aquellas heverlas recibido, ni essas haverlas
trahido de californias. El año passado despues de haver
dado las mulas à las missiones se quedava con mas cien
mulas, y ahora quando vino con el P. Presidente para lle-
varse viveres para las Escoltas trajo unas pocas y quisi
la mitad eran de las missiones, y haviendole dicho que
las mulas que trahia eran muy pocas para carrear
los dichos viveres, respondió que ya se compondria con
las mulas de la Mission, pues que todas eran del Rey,
de esto se sigue que en las missiones no pueden arar por
estar las mulas ocupadas en las cosas del Rey, y por con-
siguiente no poder sembrar, y tambien por no haver

por no haver trahido las mulas suficientes, se estan en la mis-
sión de Sn. Gabriel padeciendo hambre aun con la venida
de los dos Barcos. Oyde essa mission hasta al desembar-
cadero habra como legua y media, y porcausa del conti-
nuo carreo ya de llevar la agua de acá à los Barcos, y
ya de traher los viveres del Rey (cuyo carreo lo debian
hacer las mulas del Rey) han llegado à tal estado que
las mas de ellas estan matadas, y por su flaqueza en que a gran
por no poder comer pues no tienen apenas tiempo para
descansar, no pueden ya traher carga entera porque se
cayen en el camino; y assi esta especie de dotaciones que han
hecho à las missiones segun veo no son mas que de
nombre, y de cumplimientos. Veynte y cinco eran las bestias que se havian dado à essa Mission, y el Sr. Dn. Pedro
gusto lo que quiso y solamente dio aun veo por ceremo-
nias sr. mulas de carga, dos de silla, y dos de cavallos,
no se escrivo sobre este punto el como fue; porque ya supongo
que lo sabe V.R. y tambien ya se le escrive el P. Presidente
Junipero Serra.

En quanto al punto de trabajar le digo que
al año pasado se sembro un poco de trigo, y lo trabajó un
soldado de cuera, este, y un hermano suyo se havian ofreci-
do à trabajar para la Mission, y lo proprio fue oserlo el
Sr. Dn. Pedro, que los quito de acá. Les dice delante de los
Padres este cavallero, que trabajen para la mission, pero

pero segun sus obras, les dice lo contrario. Desde el mes de
marzo hasta que vinieron los Barcos dos Indios, y yo
hizimos una casa para poder meter los aceros, y este
cavallero luego que llego de Monterrey ya se enamoró
de ella, y aunque se le ofreció otra para meter sus cosas que
aunque no era tan buena, pero con la gente que tenia podia haverla remendada en quatro dias, y servirse de ella,
pero ni la quiso, ni lo hizo, sino que decia que hecharia todos los viveres en medio de la plaza, y para que no hi-
ziesse semejante disparate se le presto la casa nueva.

En todas las missiones nuevas como se supone que no hay
mas que Gentiles, y estos no saben trabajar, se habria de
dar un Arriero para manejar las mulas, un vaquero
y algunos para trabajar al campo, y enseñar los Christianos nuevos à trabajar; pero en ninguna de essas no se
hà dado mas que un Arriero, y este lo quita el Sr. Dn Pedro
quando se le antoja, y nos quedamos sin Arriero Vaquero
y todo lo demas conque se pudiera adelantar la Mission
y es preciso que los Padres sepan el arte general del Be-
ato Raymundo, porque sino, nos quedamos con nada.

En quanto al punto de los Indios digo que se adelantaria
muchissimo si huviera que comer, y buen exemplo de
parte de los Soldados: de comer no se les puede dar nada
porque lo que hà dado el Sr Dn Pedro no basta para la

para la mitad del año para los Indios de Californias que
hay acà, y assi poco se adelantarà en el presente estado.

El exemplo de parte de los Soldados, no hay duda que hay
algunos que lo tienen, y merecen qualquier atencion, pero son muchissimos que merecerian una horca, por
los continuos desatinos que cometen cogiendo, y violentan-
do mugeres. No hay Mission alguna endonde no hayan
escandalizado todos los Gentiles, y aun en los caminos
segun me han dicho, se conòce claramente segun expresan
los mismos Gentiles, que estan haciendo mil maldades,
y con particularidad en el septo, han hecho instancia de
estos puntos al Sr. Dn Pedro los Padres, y este Sr. hà hecho
muy poco caso de esto. Algunos hà castigado, pero luego
que le prometian que trabajarian en el presidio, los
soltava, esto hacia en el año pasado, pero ahora ni los castiga, ni les dice nada en quanto en este punto. Supongo
que algunos Ministros le escriviràn cada uno respectiva-
mente de su Mission, y assi no paso à decirle los casos
que han sucedido en otras Missiones, solamente habla-
rè de essa de Sn Diego.

En una de essas rancharias cerca-
nay à essa mission de Sn Diego, laqual ranchaxia es muy
grande, y està enel camino que và à monterrey, los Gentiles de ella han estado muchas veces para venir acà à
matarnos à todos, y el motivo de esso hàsido, porque fueron
allà unos soldados, y cogieron sus mugeres, y otros solda-

soldados que ivan de correo à Monterrey metieron las bestias dentro sus semillas, y se les comieron. Tres rancharias mas que hay vecinas de acà como, legua, o, legua y media, me han hecho varias instancias de lo mismo; por este motivo algunas veces que el P. Francisco Guemes, ò yo hemos ido à ver ysas rancharias, lo propio ha sido vernos que escapase de su rancharia, y se ivan, o, los montes, o en los rincones y solamente sequedava en las ranchariaes algunos hombres, y algunas mugeres muy viejas; me han dicho los Christianos de acà, que muchos de los Gentiles de las ya apresadas rancharias, depan sus casitas, y sus semillas que cogen en las tierras de sus rancharias, y se van à los montes padesciendo hambre, y esto lo hacen porque los soldados no les cojan sus mugeres por los muchos exemplares que tienen ya.

Estos Indios de acà aunque en el principio de la fundaccion de la mission se manifestaron malos no es de admirar; lo primero, porque ellos no sabian paraque havian venido, sino que pensavan que les querian quitar sus tierras. Ahora ya todos quieren ser christianos porque ya saben que hay un Dios, que este hizo el cielo, la tierra, y todas las cosas, que hay Infierno, y Gloria, que tienen alma etc. pero no en el principio de la fundacion nada de esso sabian, sino que pensaban que eran assi mismo como los irracionales; y quando vinieron los Barcos al principio, que veian, que los mas

se morian, con muchissima repugnancia rezavan, y de
ninguna manera querian ser Chriptianos, sino que de-
cian que ser Chriptiano era malo, y luego se morian, y
no es de admirar que dipieran esso quando veian, que
los mas de los marineros, è, Indios de Californias se
morian, pero ahora ya gracias à Dios los hà convertido Dios
de unos saulos, à unos Pablos, Todos ellos conocen los pre-
ceptos naturales, y estos, segun estoy informado los han
guardado siempre tan bien o, mejor que los Christianos de muchas partes. Ellos no tienen Idolos, no tienen
borracheras, ni se casan con parientes, y mugeres una
solamente tienen, Los casados con la suya, y no mas
los solteros duermen juntos, y apartados de mugeres
y casados, y si alguno juega con la muger que no es
suya, es reñido, y castigado de sus capitanes. De los
de Californias hè oido y decir que son dados à este vi-
cio del septo, pero los de acà no pude averiguar falta
alguna en essa materia. En los primeros Adultos que bau-
tizamos, quando les enseñaba que el coger la muger con
quien no estaba casada era malo, me dixeron, que ya
lo sabian, y que entre ellos lo tenian por muy malo, y
assi de ninguna manera lo hacian; Los soldados me dixeron son Christianos, y sabiendo que Dios los castiga al
Infierno lo hacen cogiendo nuestras mugeres, nosotros dixeron aunque no sabiamos que Dios castigaba por esso
el Infierno lo teniamos por muy malo, y no lo haciamos
y menos ahora sabiendo que el Dios nos hade castigar si lo hacemos

60

3

Lo propio fué oir esso que me soltaron las lagrimas
al ver que unos Gentiles hayā de dar el exemplo à los
Chrissianos. Entre los muchos casos que ha havido en
essa Mission solamente diré dos que son muy neces-
sarios que V. R. los sepa, y con particularidad el ulti-
mo, que diré.

      Un dia como à los primeros de Agosto
del presente año de 1772 fui à la ranchería mas
immediata à la Mission, que estarà lexos de essa como cinquenta passos; y me dixeron los Indios Chrissianos: Padre aqui està una muger que no està
casada, y està preñada; pues como y esso les dixé: no,
he me haveis dicho tantas veces que ninguno coge la muger que no es suya? Es verdad Padre me dixeron, que no
lo hacemos, ni lo hemos hecho alguno de nosotros con esta
muger, sino que pué dice la muger; que viniendo de la
ranchería del rincon (Jaqual ranchería está de essa
Mission como legua y media) la cogieron el soldado
Hernandez, y el soldado llamado Bravo, y pecaron
con ella, y aunque ella se escapaba, pero como es quasi
ciega, no podia correr mucho, y por esso està assi sin
estar casada; y me dixeron mas, que ella se estava afren-
tada de estar assi, sin estar casada, y que por esso havia
hecho muchas diligencias para abortar, y no puedo,
pero que luego que nacerà la criatura, la mataria.

+ y el soldado
Juliano Murillo

Le dijé por el intérprete (que aunque yo algo la entendía
pero paraque ella lo entendiera mejor me servi del Intérprete) que no hiciera semejante disparate, que Dios la ha-
vía de castigar al Infierno, que espera el chiquito, y le
daríamos ropa para vestirle, y lo bautizaríamos. En
varias veces le hize estas y otras exortacciones, para
que desára de executar sus malas intencios; pero nada deesso valió, sino que quando vino el tiempo de
parir sufué à la ranchería ya espresada del rincon
en donde parió, y mató la criatura, sin poderla yo
bautizar. El matar la criatura sucedió à media-
nos de Agosto de este año. Me dijeron los Indios que
vieron el muchachito, que era blanquito y todas sus
muestras indicavan que era hijo de los soldados.

Segundo caso.

Dia 11 de Septiembre del presente año fuerô à la ranchería llamada del Corral los soldados Castelo, Juan
Maria Ruiz, Bravo, y otro que su nombre no lo
sabian los Indios, pero si bien lo conocian de cara; y
un Marinero llamado Ignacio Marques, y habiendo
llegado à dicha ranchería, pidieron à las Indias, Tunay
las que le dieron graciosamente, y luego pidieron les
diessen ollas, y no queriendo darselas se adelantó el soldado Castelo à tomarlas con violencia delante de dicho
Marinero Marques; y usando de alguna llaneza en
coger de la mano à una Muger, se separó de los sol-

soldados el oppresado marinero, dando à entender no quería cooperar à tanta iniquidad como ivan à executar los dichos soldados, y de facto executaron, luego que el dicho se apartò de ellos.

Antes pues de pecar los dichos soldados con las mugeres, el Soldado Castelo, y el Soldado Bravo amenazaron à un Indio Chrisiano llamado Jose Antonio que se hallava en dicha ranchería, paraque nada manifestasse de lo que veía. Llevo el soldado Castelo una muger Gentil à un corral que sirve de trinchera à la ranchería, y dentro el corral cogiò el dicho soldado la muger, y pecò con ella haciendola violentada; saliò el dicho soldado, y entrò en el mismo corral el soldado Juan Maria Ruiz, y pecò con la misma muger; despues de esto soltaron la muger, y se fueron à la ranchería, y el soldado cuyo nombre no se sabe cogiò otra muger con violencia y la llevò dentro el mismo corral, y allí pecò, saliò este, y entrò el soldado Bravo, y pecò con ella, saliò este y entrò el soldado Juan Maria Ruiz, è hizo lo mismo saliò este, y entro el soldado Castelo, y executò lo mismo fueronse à la ranchería, y el soldado Castelo diò à essa ultima muger dos torillas, y algunas cintas de ropa colorada; à essa misma muger diò tambien algunas cintas de ropa el soldado Juan Maria Ruiz, à la primera muger tambien le dieron algunas cintas de ropa estos dos dichos soldados.

✝

Paraque estas fatalidades no se supieran, los soldados Castelo, y Bravo dijeron al Indio Jose Antonio (que es ya
arriba espresado) el qual estuvo en la ranchería todo el
tiempo de la función) que si avisavan al Padre lo havian de cassigar. Llegó acá en la Mission el dicho Jose
Antonio, y el soldado Castelo le dió dos tortillas, diciendole que no avisara.

En el mismo dia por la tarde vi-
nieron las dos mugeres à avisarme de lo que havia pa-
à la mission sado, las que entraron llorando, y fueron vistas de muchos
soldados que estavan dentro, y presumiendome el por-
que venian las despaché à la ranchería immediata à
la mission, paraque publicamente no se supiera el caso,
hiví à la ranchería pasado algun rato, y me informé
de todo lo dicho de las mismas mugeres con quienes havian pecado los dichos soldados, sirviendome de inter-
prete para mayor claridad Diego Ribera que es el que
me sirve para enseñar la Doctrina Christiana.

De este
caso me informé dos veces con las dos dichas mugeres,
y con el dicho Indio Jose Antonio tres veces, y unos, y
otros siempre convinieron con lo mismo. De essa
maldad se siguió otra, que abisus abisum invocat, y
fue: que este mesmo Indio que me havia avisado de esse
caso, lo pusieron al cepo sin avisarme, y yo lo saqué
a contraposición del cabo, del cepo, porque juzgué que

12

juzgue con fundamento alguno le ivan à castigar, paraque no confesara la verdad del dicho caso. Nô te escrivo el caso todo segun las circunstancias, porque el P.
Presidente Junipero Serra se lo lleva escrito segun todas
las circunstancias. Lo que suplico à V.R. es que haga todo lo possible (como supongo lo harà) paraque no se pierda
o, no se atraze essa conquista por causa del mal exemplo
de estos mestizos, como y tambien se componga en lo temporal. Pido en la memoria un reloxito de sol de todas alturas, uno como el que mandò V.R. se hiziera para el P. Antonio Paterna quando estava en la Sierra-
gorda; estimarè de V.R. lo mande hacer, o, buscarlo.

Vâ dentro este pliego la memoria de los Padres de la
Mission de Sn Luis Obispo que por haverse descuy-
dado de ponerla dentro sus pliegos me la remitieron,
paraque dentro de mis pliegos la embiara à V.R.
y me quedo como siempre todo de V.R. rogando à
Dios me lo guarde, y conserve Ms As en su divino amor
y gracia desde essa Mission de Sn Diego, y octubre 17
de 1772

B.L.M. de V.R. su siempre afectissimo amigo
seguro, y humilde Subdito
Fr Luis Jayme

Fr. Luis Jayme

Lo mataron los Yndios, y
estando incado de rodillas
les dixo antes de morir
entre otras palabras, Hijos
amar á Dios, y cogiendo uno
de los Yndos, una piedra
grande, se la dexó caér
sobre la Cabeza, diciendole,
Ya no hay amar á Dios. Con
lo que finalizó, el dichoso
Pe. su vida Apostolica.

*700 copies printed by
Grant Dahlstrom at the
Castle Press
Pasadena, California
1970*